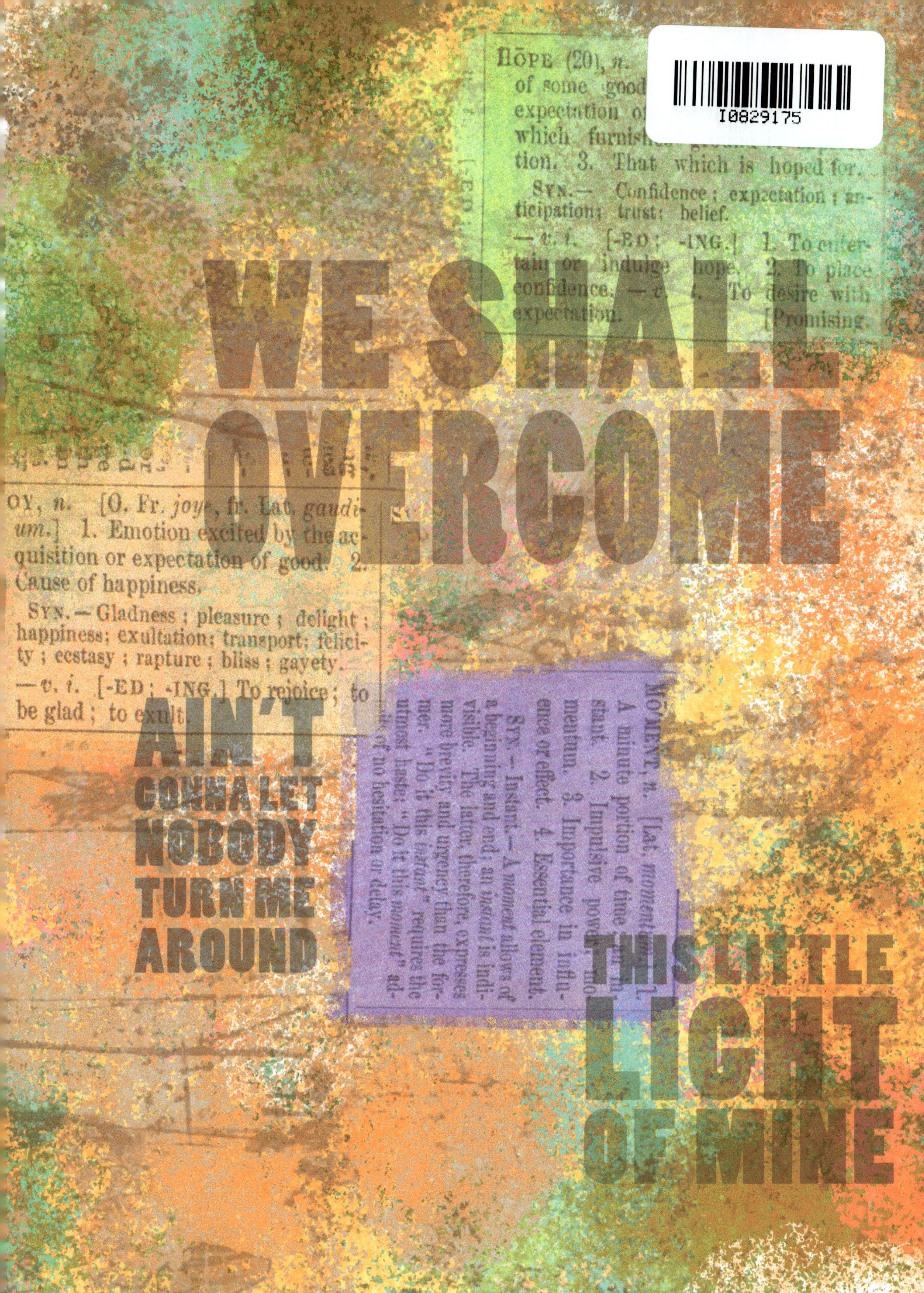

WE SHALL OVERCOME
AIN'T GONNA LET NOBODY TURN ME AROUND
THIS LITTLE LIGHT OF MINE
HOPE (20), n.
of some good
expectation of
which furnishes
tion. 3. That which is hoped for.
SYN.— Confidence; expectation; anticipation; trust; belief.
—v.t. [-ED; -ING.] 1. To entertain or indulge hope. 2. To place confidence. —v.t. To desire with expectation. [Promising.
OY, n. [O. Fr. joye, fr. Lat. gaudium.] 1. Emotion excited by the acquisition or expectation of good. 2. Cause of happiness.
SYN.—Gladness; pleasure; delight; happiness; exultation; transport; felicity; ecstasy; rapture; bliss; gayety.
—v.i. [-ED; -ING.] To rejoice; to be glad; to exult.
I0829175

This book is dedicated to all the beautiful souls that I call family and friends who let their lights shine daily.

To Lori, Harriet, Elliot, and Karen, thank you from the bottom of my heart. --V.N.

Published in paperback 2022 by

Blue Apple Books

South Orange, New Jersey

www.blueapplebooks.com

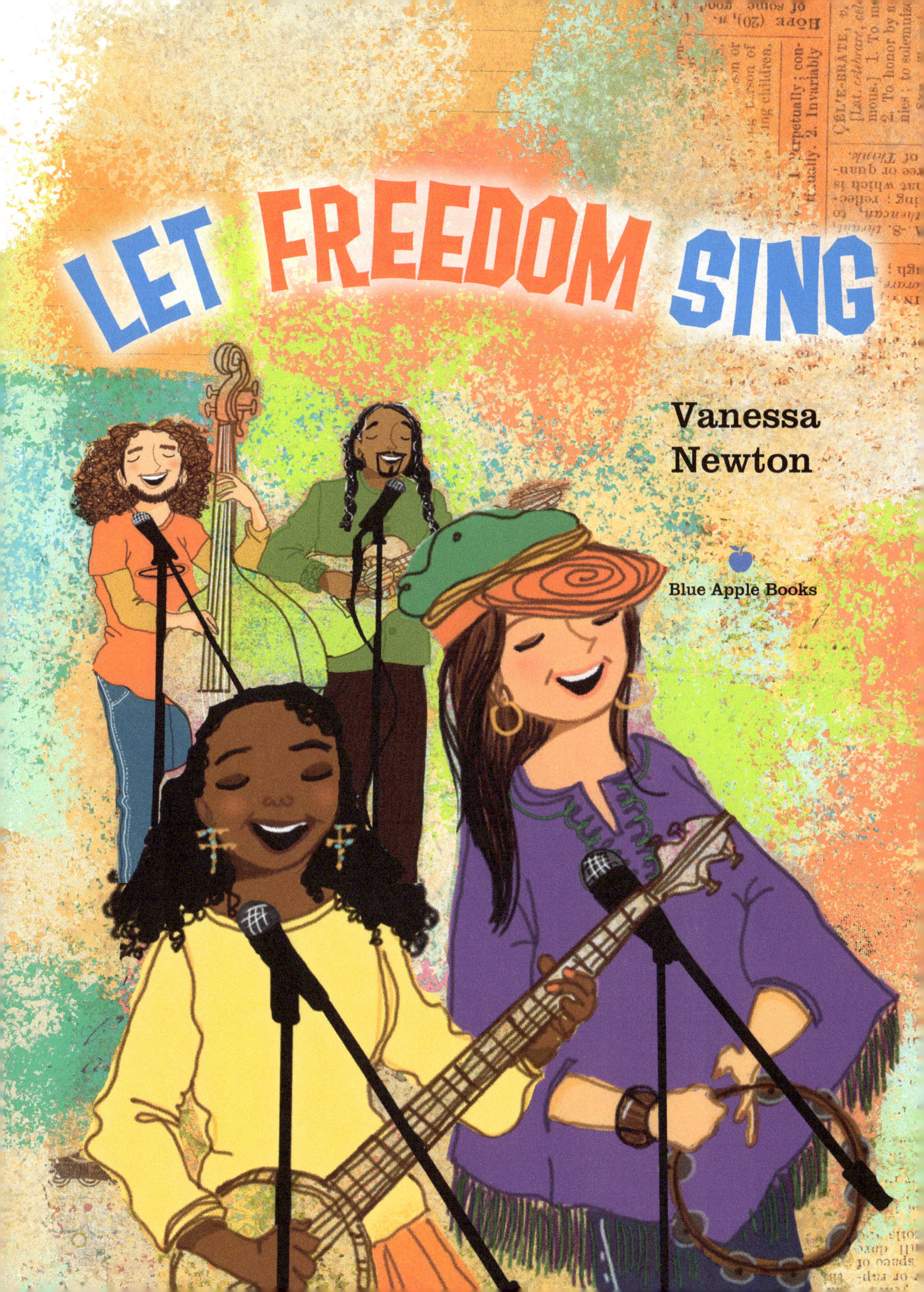
LET FREEDOM SING
Vanessa
Newton
Blue Apple Books

FREEDOM SINGS!

Powerful. Inspirational. Unifying. Music was an undeniable force in the Civil Rights movement in the 1950's and 1960's. At marches, at meetings, at demonstrations, songs motivated activists who were expressing their desire for freedom and equality. Many of the protest songs were African-American spirituals, their lyrics adapted to speak about the hardships black Americans faced day in, day out.

Again and again these songs were sung—in Montgomery, Greensboro, Little Rock, New Orleans, Selma, and Washington, D.C.—all over the South where scores of people gathered, fighting for change.

They sang about boycotting buses...

**If you miss me at the back of the bus*
If you can't find me back there
Come on up to the front of the bus
I'll be sittin right there

sitting at lunch counters...

**I'm gonna sit at the Woolworth counter,*
I'm gonna sit at the Woolworth counter one of these days

marching for equal rights...

**Will you march for your rights?*
"Certainly, Lord."
Will you march for your rights?
"Certainly, Lord."

serving time in jail...

**Ain't gonna let no jailhouse*
Turn me 'roun
I'm gonna keep on walkin'
Keep on talkin'
Walkin' into freedom land

attending school...

**If you can't find me in the school room*
If you can't find me in there
Come on out to the picket line
I'll be standing right there

standing ground...

**We're fighting for our rights and*
We shall not be moved
Just like a tree that's planted by the water,
We shall not be moved

overcoming all odds...

**We shall overcome,*
We shall overcome
We shall overcome someday
Oh-o deep in my heart
I do believe
We shall overcome someday

and letting the best in themselves shine the brightest...

**This little light of mine,*
I'm going to let it shine.
Let it shine, let it shine, let it shine.

Rosa Parks did.

This Little Light of Mine captured the spirit and heart of the movement. A gospel children's song written by Harry Dixon Loes, it became an anthem of the time thanks to the efforts of civil rights activists Zilphia Horton and Fannie Lou Hamer.

** If You Miss Me at the Back of the Bus; I'm Gonna Sit at the Welcome Table; Certainly Lord; Ain't Gonna Let Nobody Turn Me 'Round; If You Miss Me at the Back of the Bus; We Shall Not be Moved; We Shall Overcome; This Little Light of Mine*

Confronted with dehumanizing indignities and daily sacrifices, each person had to find their inner strength and resolve – their inner light.

Dr. Martin Luther King, Jr. did.

Ernest Green did.

Elizabeth Eckford did.

Jefferson Thomas did.

Terrence Roberts did.

Carlotta Walls did.

Minnijean Brown did.

Gloria Ray did.

Thelma Mothershed did.

Melba Pattillo did.

Ezell A. Blair Jr. did.

David Richmond did.

Joseph McNeil did.

Franklin McCain did.

Ruby Bridges did.

Lyndon B. Johnson did.

Barack Obama did.

They and many others, unnamed and unsung, let their lights shine.

From the editors at Blue Apple Books

This little light of mine,

I’m gonna let it shine.

This little light of mine,
I'm going to let it shine.

This little light of mine,
I'm going to let it shine.

Let it shine!

Let it shine!

Let it shine!

On benches just for 'colored,'
Black folks obeyed the rules.

Rosa Parks refused to move,
She let her light shine.

Preaching from his pulpit,
Dr. King had a dream.

When he spoke in Alabama,
He let his light shine.

DECEMBER 4,
1955

DECEMBER 5,
1955
—
DECEMBER 21,
1956

With boycotts in Montgomery,
Dr. King inspired all.

Walkers along the bus routes,
They let their lights shine.

time as she went dow
what was going to h
down and make out w

This little light of mine,
I'm going to let it shine.

This little light of mine,
I'm going to let it shine.

This little light of mine,
I'm going to let it shine.

Let it shine!

Let it shine!

Let it shine!

SEPTEMBER 23, 1957

The Little Rock Nine:
Ernest Green, Elizabeth Eckford, Jefferson Thomas, Gloria Ray, Terrence Roberts, Carlotta Walls, Minnijean Brown, Melba Pattillo, Thelma Mothershed,

Schools for blacks in Little Rock,
Separate, but not equal.

Nine high school kids,
They let their lights shine.

FEBRUARY 1,
1960
The Greensboro Four:
Ezell A. Blair Jr., David Richmond,
Joseph McNeil, Franklin McCain
Maggie

Students at lunch counters—
They hoped to be served.

As the Greensboro Four sat waiting,
They let their lights shine.

NOVEMBER 14, 1960

At a school in New Orleans,
Shouting filled the air.

Ruby Bridges walked alone.
She let her light shine.

This little light of mine,
I'm going to let it shine.

This little light of mine,
I'm going to let it shine.

This little light of mine,
I'm going to let it shine.

Let it shine!

Let it shine!

Let it shine!

AUGUST 28, 1963

At the March on Washington,
Thousands walked for miles.

Dr. King had a dream.
He let his light shine.

President Lyndon Johnson
Helped to change the law.

Civil rights for everyone.
He let his light shine.

JANUARY 20, 2009

Speaking to all Americans,
Barack Obama had a dream.

As President of the United States,
He let his light shine.

This little light of mine,
I'm going to let it shine.

This little light of mine,
I'm going to let it shine.

This little light of mine,
I'm going to let it shine.

Let it shine! Let it shine!

Let it SHINE!

I'M GONNA SIT AT THE WELCOME TABLE

DREAM, *n.* [Icel. *draumr.* Cf. A.-S. *dream*, joy, gladness.] 1. Series of thoughts of a person in sleep. 2. An idle fancy; a revery. —*v. i.* [-ED or -T; -ING.] 1. To have images in the mind, in sleep. 2. To indulge in idle revery; to imagine. —*v. t.* To imagine in a dream, or in an analogous state.

WE SHALL NOT BE MOVED

CERTAINLY LORD

Vanessa Newton was only three when she found a box of crayons and wished to be an artist. She used many surfaces such as canvases, white walls and the sides of the kitchen stove. Vanessa is largely self-taught, though she has attended art school in New York. She lives in East Orange, New Jersey with her husband, their seven-year-old daughter, and a fat cat

IF YOU MISS ME AT THE BACK OF THE BUS

RE-MEM'BER, *v. t.* [-ED; -ING.] [Lat. *rememorare*; *re*, again, and *memorare*, to bring to remembrance.] 1. To bring to mind again; to recall.

www.ingramcontent.com/pod-product-compliance
Lightning Source LLC
LaVergne TN
LVHW060643110826
845147LV00018B/1033

* 9 7 8 1 6 0 9 0 5 6 8 4 1 *